RESURRECTION BAY

by Leah Kaminski

CHERRY LAKE PUBLISHING • ANN ARBOR, MICHIGAN

Published in the United States of America by:

CHERRY LAKE PRESS

2395 South Huron Parkway, Suite 200, Ann Arbor, MI 48104
www.cherrylakepublishing.com

Reading Adviser: Marla Conn MS, Ed., Literacy specialist, Read-Ability, Inc.

Series Adviser: Amy Reese, Coordinator of Elementary Science; Howard County School
System, MD; President of Maryland Science Supervisors Association

Book Design: Book Buddy Media

Photo Credits: ©Mai Vu/Getty Images, background, ©mhgstan/Shutterstock, cover (bottom left), ©iStockphoto/
Getty Images, cover (lined paper), ©sethakan/Getty Images, cover, ©Rainer Lesniewski/Getty Images, cover (map),
©DenisTangneyJr/Getty Images, cover (back), ©Pixabay, cover (red circle), ©Anne Lindgren/Getty Images, cover (bottom
right), ©Devanath/Pixabay, cover (paperclips), ©louanapires/Pixabay, cover (paper texture), ©JonnyNoTrees/Getty
Images, 1, ©GlobalP/Getty Images, 3 (left), ©BDMcIntosh/Getty Images, 3 (right), ©Joesboy/Getty Images, 4, ©Hey
Darlin/Getty Images, 6, ©Paresh Saxena/Getty Images, 7, ©John Pennell/Getty Images, 8, ©Feng Wei Photography/Getty
Images, 9, ©PatrickCivello/Getty Images, 9, ©Crystal Eye Studio/Shutterstock, 10, ©Mike Tiffany Ritz/Shutterstock, 11,
©MH Anderson Photography/Shutterstock, 12, ©sarkophoto/Getty Images, 13, ©Clemens Stockner/Wikimedia, 14,
©Saddako/Getty Images, 15 (top), ©LaraBelova/Getty Images, 15 (bottom), ©OVasik/Getty Images, 16, ©AlbertoLoyo/
Getty Images, 17, ©wwing/Getty Images, 18, ©ian600f/Getty Images, 19, ©Jennifer Idol/Stocktrek Images/Getty Images, 20,
©Peter Stevens/Flickr, 21 (top), ©narvikk/Getty Images, 22 (bottom), ©johnandersonphoto/Getty Images, 23, ©Mariusz
S. Jurgielevwicz/Shutterstock, 2 , ©gilbert/Wikimedia, 25, ©Rawpixel/Getty Images, 26, ©Lovas50/Shutterstock, 27

Library of Congress Cataloging-in-Publication Data has been filed and is available at catalog.loc.gov

Cherry Lake Publishing would like to acknowledge the work of the Partnership for 21st Century Learning, a
Network of Battelle for Kids. Please visit *http://www.battelleforkids.org/networks/p21* for more information.

Printed in the United States of America
Corporate Graphics

CHERRY LAKE PRESS

CONTENTS

CHAPTER 1

The Systems of Resurrection Bay

From the southwest coast of Alaska juts the large Kenai Peninsula. Several bays cut dramatically into the high cliffs of the peninsula's southeastern coast. These long, narrow, deep **inlets** are called fjords. Fjords are spaces between high mountains or cliffs. They are filled with water. Resurrection Bay is a fjord.

Air, water, earth, and living creatures interact to create a thriving system in this fjord. The air above the bay is called its **atmosphere**. The water itself is the **hydrosphere**. The land surrounding it is called its **geosphere**. The plants and animals are its **biosphere**.

Glaciers created the shoreline of Resurrection Bay. They once covered land more than 50 miles (80 kilometers) past the current coast. The soft surface of the land was carved away. This left steep, polished rock walls and deep valleys. The ice melted. Valleys filled with water. These became fjords. Because a fjord is a water-filled valley, the water becomes deep very quickly off Resurrection Bay's shoreline.

* Even in warm seasons, ice covers much of the Kenai Mountains that surround the bay.

Glaciers are still important to the area. Resurrection Bay receives a lot of water from glaciers. There is an icefield high in the Kenai Mountains. It is called the Harding Icefield. An icefield is a large area of connected glaciers. Bear Glacier is one large glacier in the Harding Icefield. It flows down a valley, creating an ice-filled **lagoon** along the way.

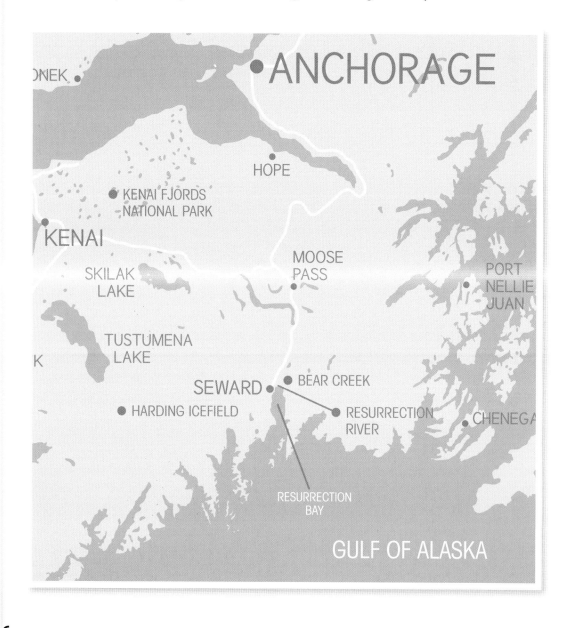

Resurrection Bay is not just a fjord. It is also an **estuary**. In an estuary, freshwater from the land meets saltwater from the ocean. When the freshwater enters the bay, it changes the speed of the water currents. It also changes their direction. This mixing affects **nutrient** and **sediment** levels. The water of Resurrection Bay is generally high in nutrients. It is cold, but it remains mostly free of ice in winter. The somewhat salty water freezes at a lower temperature than freshwater would.

This area of Alaska receives only six hours of sunlight in the darkest part of winter. It receives 19 hours in the longest days of summer. Summers in Resurrection Bay are cool. Winters are mild and wet. Average high summer temperatures are around 60 degrees Fahrenheit (16 degrees Celsius). Average low winter temperatures are 20°F (–7°C). Seward is the bay's main city. It receives 64 inches (163 centimeters) of rain and 75 inches (191 cm) of snow per year. The mountains receive even more snow. Harding Icefield receives an average of 400 inches (1,016 cm).

A small city of less than 3,000 people, Seward is the only city on the bay.

The bay and its surrounding land contain many **habitats**, or homes for plants and animals. These include islands and **tundra**. The water habitats are affected by glacial runoff. When glaciers melt, this water runs into the bay. In the mountains is a very **fertile** region of rainforest. It has some of the greatest **biomass** of any rainforest in the world.

The rainforest stretches along the Pacific coast from Northern California up to Alaska.

The Harding Icefield

The Harding Icefield is one of only four icefields left in the nation. It is the largest that is only within U.S. land. It contains glaciers such as Exit and Lowell Glaciers. It covers more than 700 square miles (1,813 square km). In the icefield is Truuli Peak. This peak is 6,612 feet (2,015 meters) above sea level. The Harding Icefield is probably a mile (1.6 km) deep at some points. It once covered most of the peninsula. That was 23,000 years ago. It has been slowly melting for about 10,000 years. It is melting faster now because of global **climate change**.

CHAPTER 2

The Resurrection Bay Watershed

A watershed is the land that drains freshwater into a bay. In most watersheds, rain and snowmelt flow over the land and into rivers. The rivers flow into the bay. In Resurrection Bay, the watershed also contains glaciers. Nearly half of the freshwater flowing into the bay every year comes from glaciers. Glaciers cover nearly a quarter of the Resurrection Bay watershed.

Watershed Diagram

The land around Resurrection Bay contains many glaciers, streams, and rivers. These drain into the bay. The Harding Icefield and **wetlands** at lower elevations are some of the most important water sources in the bay's watershed.

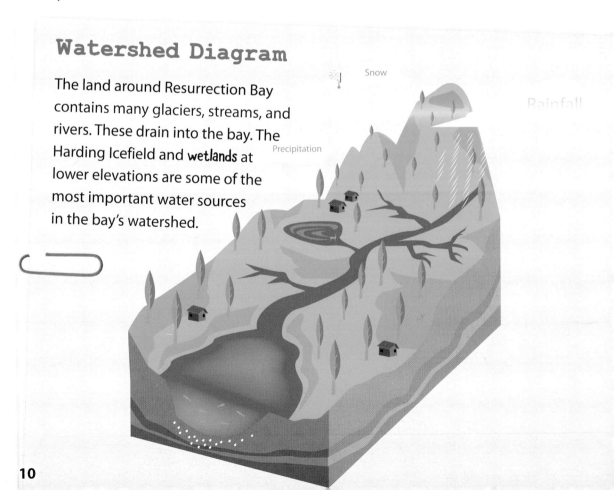

Snow

Rainfall

Precipitation

Resurrection River is the most important river of Resurrection Bay's watershed. It drains partly from glaciers in the Harding Icefield. The river flows through a steep, deep valley. It ends in a **delta** by the bay. Another very important water source is the stream flowing along the edge of Bear Glacier. It begins at **nunataks** in the icefield. It drains many **wetlands** along the way too.

The Resurrection River flows 32 miles (51.5 km) from the mountains to the bay.

Glacial rivers are always cold. They are always high in oxygen. Oxygen is an element in air and water. It is necessary for plant and animal life. Water from glacial rivers makes the bay water cold and high in oxygen. It also makes the water fresher. These streams fill the bay with sediment and nutrients. As they flow into the bay, they cause deeper bay water to well up. This deeper water has its own nutrients.

By introducing and mixing nutrients, glacial water from the watershed allows bay life to flourish. In the spring, glaciers melt more quickly. This increases the nutrients flowing to the bay. The water is mixed by the entering glacial runoff, and by strong winds and currents.

Along with more sunlight, this combination creates a spring bloom of tiny plants. These plants are called phytoplankton. Phytoplankton blooms in spring and summer. It turns the water of the bay a deep green color. Many larger plants and animals depend on the phytoplankton.

* Resurrection River is very popular for salmon fishing.

* Building too many structures too near the bay contributes to the problem of runoff.

The watershed affects the bay's health in good and bad ways. For example, as more buildings fill the land of the watershed, harmful runoff may increase. This occurs when water collects chemicals and other contaminants from land. Water drains faster when there are too many roads and hard surfaces. The land cannot filter the water. Runoff drains into the bay, filling it with contaminants. What happens on the land affects the bay.

CHAPTER 3

Plants and Animals of Resurrection Bay

There are many unique habitats in Resurrection Bay and its watershed. Many different plants live on the highest peaks and in the lowest depths. Nunataks support grasses that feed mountain goats. Alpine tundra plants grow a little lower. Alder and willow grow below the tundra. They are in what is called a transition zone.

* Nunataks are also called "glacial islands." The word nunatak comes from Greenland.

Forested areas in the Kenai Peninsula are usually below 1,500 feet (457 m). Much of the area's forest is part of the largest **temperate** rainforest on Earth. The rainforest is filled with Sitka spruce trees. Sitka spruce are some of the tallest trees on Earth. They can live for 700 years. Western hemlock and lots of moss and lichen also grow in the rainforest.

* Black bears can actually be blonde, cinnamon, and even blue.

Shoreline wetlands and beaches have plants such as beach rye and goose tongue. Goose tongue is a favorite spring food for bears. Rocky cliffs have tufts of grasses. Puffins fertilize these plants with their nests.

Cold, northern ocean water is very friendly to animals. Resurrection Bay's water is calm. The cold, calm water brings many animals to the area. Marine worms, insects, and clams live in the mud on the bay's bottom. Fiddler crabs and sea cucumbers feed on decaying animals. Five **species** of Pacific salmon swim there. These are Chinook, coho, sockeye, pink, and chum. In the summer, tens of thousands of sockeye salmon travel miles up the rivers. They make this journey before laying their eggs.

Sockeye are also called red salmon. They are red during spawning, though they are blue while in the ocean.

* Orcas, or killer whales, eat many silver salmon in the bay. This whale is at the top of the food chain in the fjords.

Many larger sea animals also live in the bay. Some of these are sea otters, harbor and northern fur seals, orcas, and porpoises. They swim, eat, and rest in the water and on the bay's islands. Steller sea lions eat up to 120 pounds (54 kilograms) of fish per day. The Gulf of Alaska's current provides a **migrating** path for humpback, grey, killer, and other whales. All of these whales visit the bay in spring. They come to eat the blooms of plankton.

Many land mammals live there too. Mountain goats and Dall's sheep live in the alpine tundra. Wolves, caribou, and moose roam through the rainforests. There are also smaller animals, like porcupines and red squirrels. Brown and black bears eat from streams full of spawning salmon. They eat greens and seaweed on the beach.

More than 100 types of seabirds and shorebirds live on and near the water of Resurrection Bay. Black oystercatchers with bright orange bills live on open beaches. Kittiwakes and gulls fly overhead. Common murres and cormorants float on the water. Tufted and horned puffins huddle in tufts of grass on the cliffs. The horned puffin has a thick bill. It can hold a dozen small fish at once.

Mountain goats actually belong to the antelope family. Their hooves have two toes that allow them to move confidently in rocky mountains.

* The goshawk eats many small animals and even other birds. It is hunted by bald eagles and large animals like bears.

Goshawks and bald eagles nest in forests. So do 50 species of songbirds. These include chickadees, nuthatches, thrushes, and warblers. Ground-nesting birds like juncos live in mossy bogs. Wetlands harbor rare species such as trumpeter swans. Mountain streams are home to American dippers and harlequin ducks. All of these plant and animal species are connected. The health of one affects the health of all.

CHAPTER 4

Changing Climate, Changing Plant Life

Phytoplankton is a very important food for the animals of the fjord. Kelp and other forms of **algae** also grow in the bay. These and other **aquatic vegetation** filter the bay's water. They keep it clean and clear. Birds eat them. Young fish hide in them.

Beds of giant kelp may be called forests, but this huge algae does not have roots. It can live up to 7 years in the right environment.

The bay's plants are still healthy and growing as they should. The high amount of nutrients in the bay allows many plants to thrive. But increases in land use may affect their habitats. Global climate change is also a concern.

Algae occurs naturally in the bay. But there can be too much of it. Algae can grow too much when the water warms. It uses too much oxygen and chokes out other species. Toxic, or harmful, algae can even grow and kill wildlife. This has already happened in areas of the Kenai Peninsula. Someday, it may happen in Resurrection Bay itself.

* Toxic algae overgrowth is referred to as a "bloom" because it can be many colors, including red and green.

Almost half of Resurrection Bay's freshwater is from glacial runoff. Nutrients and sediment come from that runoff. These are very important to the growth of phytoplankton. Warming temperatures may speed up the melting of glaciers. Changes in the flow of nutrients and sediments would change the bay's water. This would affect plankton, plants, and the animals that eat them.

Alaska's cold climate has slowed the spread of **invasive species**. Most populations have not grown too large. Containing or wiping them out may still be possible. Aquatic invasive species like pike, green crabs, and tunicates are the greatest threat. Northern pike are a kind of fish. They are spreading quickly throughout Alaska. They are hungry **predators**. Pike have killed many native fish, such as rainbow trout and coho salmon. The European green crab is another dangerous predator. They eat mussels and oysters. Many birds rely on mussels and oysters. The crabs can force birds out of the bay by eating their food.

The large Northern Pike is up to 4 feet (1.2 m) long and can weigh 40 pounds (18 kg). It is native to other parts of Alaska, but is dangerous to the bay's ecosystem.

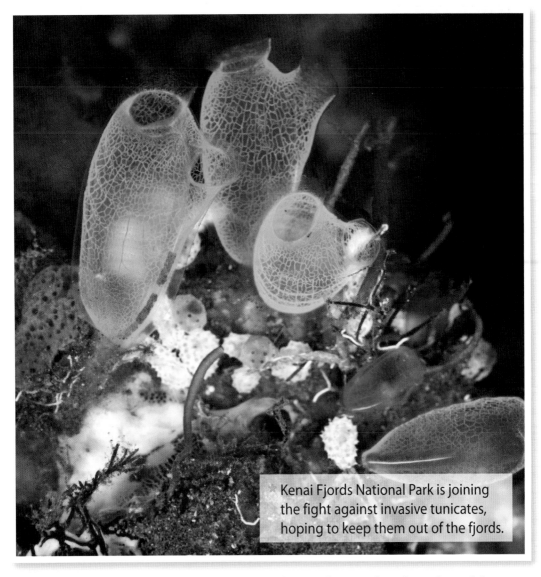

Kenai Fjords National Park is joining the fight against invasive tunicates, hoping to keep them out of the fjords.

Tunicates are a species that attach themselves to hard surfaces like rocks and piers. They take food and shelter from native species. So far, no invasive tunicate species have been found in Resurrection Bay. But they have been found elsewhere in coastal Alaska. The climate continues to change. Temperatures continue to warm. This may allow these and other invasive species to take hold in Resurrection Bay.

CHAPTER 5

Humans and the Bay

Native people in Kenai were called the Unegkurmiut. They lived there for centuries. Russians settled the land in the 1700s. They stayed on the Kenai Peninsula until 1867. By then, most native villages were already gone. The Russians used the land for wood and iron. They built ships. Later, Americans also used the land for many things. They searched for gold and mined for minerals. They built railroads, and built forts during World War II.

Fishing and tourism became the most important industries in the bay. Kenai is one of the most-visited and fastest-growing areas in Alaska. More new people move to the Kenai Peninsula every year. A higher population means more homes and businesses need to be built too.

* The last gold rush on the Kenai Peninsula ended around 1914, but tourists still like to pan for gold.

The area is still relatively unpopulated. But the population continues to grow. Threats to the environment will grow too. One major threat is loss of animal habitat. Even the increase in visitors to the Kenai Fjords National Park has already damaged habitats. Population growth can also hurt the bay's water. Fisheries, highways, airports, boats, and buildings can all increase harmful runoff and contribute to harmful algae blooms.

The Kenai Peninsula may be home to almost 64,000 people by the year 2045.

Climate change on the Kenai Peninsula is likely the biggest threat to Resurrection Bay. Yearly temperatures increased by 2 to 4°F (1.1 to 2.2°C) in 60 years. Glaciers are shrinking rapidly. The Harding Icefield and its glaciers lost 8 cubic miles (33 cubic km) in volume between the 1950s and 1990s.

Global warming causes other problems. Temperatures in non-glacial streams are too warm. This can harm salmon and their young. Pandalid shrimp are dying from warm temperatures. They are also harmed by overfishing in the bay. Climate change will probably cause changes in rainfall and snowfall patterns. This would create more flow from the watershed. The makeup of water in the bay would change too.

What Can YOU Do for the Bay?

One of the biggest threats to Resurrection Bay is climate change. Although climate change is a global problem, small changes can make a difference. People who want to reduce climate change can use less energy. This means turning off lights and appliances you aren't using, washing clothes in cold water, and using energy-saving light bulbs. People can also waste less with reusable water bottles and straws. Regular maintenance of cars helps keep harmful gases from entering the atmosphere. Finally, recycling reduces the amount of garbage in landfills, which creates gases that contribute to climate change. These small changes can help keep Resurrection Bay healthy for years to come.

Warmer temperatures also affect the land. Species in cold northern areas like Resurrection Bay are more sensitive to these changes. The forest habitat has increased. Wetlands have decreased. More than 80 percent of wetlands on the peninsula became drier between the 1950s and 1990s. The glacial habitat is changing to tundra. Warm weather also causes an increase in a harmful insect in the area. It is called the spruce bark beetle.

Spruce bark beetles have killed spruce on half of the forested acres of the Kenai Peninsula since the 1970s.

The government manages a large portion of the peninsula. Human development and pollution can hurt the bay. The government protects the bay and other fjords from these threats. Local conservation groups are trying to protect the rest of the area's habitats. For example, they are working to protect the watersheds of the peninsula from runoff.

But local efforts cannot do much about global climate change. What affects Resurrection Bay and the surrounding fjords affects the entire world. Alaskan glaciers are melting due to global climate change. This has changed sea levels more than anything else on Earth. People around the world must work on fixing this together.

Glacier Goo

Introduction

In this activity you will learn how glaciers move. These mountains of ice are made of compressed snow. They move more like honey than like something solid. They move faster when warm than when cold. The weight of new snow and ice on the top pushes glaciers downhill, creating landforms like valleys, moraines, and kettle lakes. **Gravity** makes them move down too. As they move, they bend and stretch and sometimes break.

Goo moves in a similar way to glaciers. By creating your own glaciers out of goo, you will see how these mountains of ice have shaped so much of our land as they grow, move, and shrink. Of course, unlike a glacier, goo is sticky and doesn't melt, plus you can save it to play with later!

Materials:

* Kitchen table or another flat surface that is easy to clean
* Two 8-ounce bottles of white glue
* Large mixing bowl
* Measuring cup
* Water
* Spoon
* Plastic cup
* Borax (a powdered soap found in the grocery store)
* Blue food coloring
* Cookie sheet or any kind of tray
* Gravel, dirt, rocks
* Flour
* Plastic freezer bag

Instructions:

1 Empty one bottle of white glue into a bowl. Fill the empty bottle halfway with warm water, put the cap on, and shake. Pour this gluey water into the bowl and mix with a spoon.

2 Pour ½ cup (118 milliliters) of warm water into the plastic cup. Add a heaping teaspoon (about 6 grams) of Borax. Stir. Don't worry if all the powder doesn't dissolve.

3 While stirring, slowly add the Borax water to the bowl of glue. You will feel the mixture start to thicken and connect. Once it's thick, mix with your hands. Keep adding Borax until the texture is like silly putty and you can roll it like dough. Put it on the table and let it rest.

4 Repeat those steps to make your second batch of goo—but this time, add about 10 drops of blue food coloring to your glue mixture first.

5 Now, combine the blue and white batches together. Have fun. Twist, pinch, and fold the batches together until combined in swirls and patches.

6 Lay the goo on a sheet or tray. Prop up one end of the tray to create a "mountain" for the goo glacier to flow down. Watch the shapes it creates.

7 Next time, place various sizes of rocks and dirt on the cookie sheet as obstacles for your glacier. Depending on the size of the rock, it may be picked up and carried downhill, or the glacier may flow around it.

8 Try the same with flour. Coat the surface with a layer of flour. What happens as the goo moves down? It might create hills in front of it, ridges on its side, or streaks in the flour. These are all things that glaciers can do to land too.

9 When you're done playing, place your goo in a plastic bag for safekeeping.

Glossary

algae *(AL-jee)* plant-like organism that has no roots, stems, or leaves

aquatic vegetation *(uh-KWAH-tik veh-jih-TAY-shin)* plants that live in or under water

atmosphere *(AT-muhs-feer)* part of the planet made of air

biomass *(BYE-oh-mas)* the total amount of living things in an area

biosphere *(BYE-oh-sfeer)* part of the planet made of living things

climate change *(KLYE-mit CHAYNJ)* long-term change in the Earth's weather patterns

delta *(DELTUH)* low area of land where a river divides into smaller streams before reaching the ocean

estuary *(EHS-choo-air-ee)* area where a river or tributary meets the ocean

fertile *(FUR-tul)* land that is able to produce many trees and plants

geosphere *(JEE-oh-sfeer)* part of the planet made of solid ground

glaciers *(GLAY-shurz)* huge areas of very thick ice that flow slowly over land

gravity *(GRA-vih-tee)* the invisible force that pulls bodies and objects toward Earth

habitats *(HAB-ih-tats)* natural environments where a plant or animal lives

hydrosphere *(HYE-droh-sfeer)* part of the planet made of water

inlets *(IN-lets)* small areas of water going from the sea or a large lake into the surrounding land

invasive species *(in-VAY-siv SPEE-sheez)* plants or animals that are not native to an area and cause harm to other species in that area

lagoon *(luh-GOON)* small lake near or next to a larger lake or river.

migrating *(MYE-gray-ting)* moving from one habitat or region to another according to the season

nunataks *(NUHN-uh-tak)* ridges of rock above ice and snow

nutrient *(NOO-tree-int)* important chemical necessary for all living things

predators *(PREH-duh-turz)* animals that naturally hunt and eat other animals

sediment *(SED-ih-ment)* stones or sand carried in water

species *(SPEE-sheez)* group of living things that share similar characteristics

temperate *(TEM-pur-it)* relating to a moderate climate with mild temperatures

tundra *(TUHN-druh)* frozen area of land without trees, found high in the mountains and in very cold areas

wetlands *(WET-lands)* land that is saturated with water, such as marshes and swamps

For More Information

Books

Heitkamp, Kristina Lyn. *The Water Cycle.* New York, NY: Britannica, 2018.

Herman, Gail. *What Is Climate Change?* New York, NY: Penguin, 2018.

Simon, Seymour. *Icebergs & Glaciers.* New York, NY: Harper Collins, 2018.

Websites

Ducksters Education Site
https://www.ducksters.com/science/earth_science
Find kid-friendly information about earth science and related subjects.

eSchool Today
http://eschooltoday.com/pollution/water-pollution/what-is-water-pollution.html
Learn basic facts about water pollution.

Alaska Department of Fish and Game
http://www.adfg.alaska.gov/index.cfm?adfg=viewinglocations.southeastkenai
Discover details about wildlife on the southeastern Kenai Peninsula.

Index

About the Author

Leah Kaminski lives in Chicago with her husband and son. She has written other books for children, about science, geography, and culture. Leah also writes poetry, often about the natural environment—so she loves learning more about everything related to science and ecology.